Leadership and Ethics

Financial Crime Essentials

Dr Ian Messenger

Table of Contents

Leadership

Ethics

CHAPTER 1

Leadership

LEADERSHIP is a concept that has been around for centuries. But to be an effective leader, you must have a certain set of specific skills and traits. These can be developed over time if properly guided by the right mentor or coach.

Many people falsely assume that leadership is something you're born with or without altogether, which is simply untrue. Leadership skills are not innate, but they can be developed by anyone through possessing the proper knowledge and guidance. However, people also have to learn how to correctly apply these soft skills to become influential leaders, both professionally and personally.

Like all other character traits, leadership skills can be coached into any individual who has the desire and willingness to further develop themselves through education and training. And even if your genetics aren't favourable towards specific characteristics such as confidence or poise, you still need not worry because there are many ways to find success and achieve your goals in life.

Self-leadership is the ability to lead oneself effectively. It is a critical skill for anyone who wants to succeed in life, regardless of their occupation or field of interest. To be an effective self-leader, you need to have a strong understanding of what it means to lead and how to apply leadership principles and techniques to your own life. You also need to develop other soft skills, such as communication, problem-solving, and decision-making skills.

This book provides a comprehensive guide to self-leadership, leadership, and other soft skills. It teaches you how to understand the concept of self-leadership, develop it in yourself and apply it throughout your life with great effectiveness.

Leadership is the ability to motivate and guide a group of people towards a common goal. Leaders must have strong communication skills, be able to make decisions quickly, and inspire others. Good leaders are also good listeners, and they value their team's input.

Leadership is not just about making tough decisions or giving orders; it's also about creating a positive work environment where people feel supported and appreciated. A good leader establishes trust and builds relationships with their team members.

People often think of leadership as a trait that can only be learned in a formal setting like business school, but that's not always the case. Many great leaders have never received any formal training; they learned by doing. The best way to learn is to observe others and gradually take on more responsibility. There are no shortcuts to becoming a good leader; it takes time, effort, and practice.

So, what are some of the critical skills you need to be a good leader? Here are a few:

Communication: Leaders need to communicate effectively with their team members, superiors, and other stakeholders. They must express themselves clearly, and they should also be good listeners.

Problem-solving: Leaders need to think on their feet and make decisions quickly. They must be able to assess a situation, identify the problem, and then develop a solution.

Decision-making: Leaders need to have strong decision-making skills in order to be able to make quick decisions under pressure.

Leadership style: Leaders must find a leadership style that works for them. Some leaders prefer to give orders, while others prefer to delegate tasks and let their team members make decisions.

People skills: Leaders need to build relationships with their team members and other stakeholders. They should be good listeners, and they should also give constructive feedback.

Organizational skills: Leaders need to be organized and efficient to manage their time effectively.

Ethics: Leaders must always act with integrity and honesty, and they must maintain the trust of their team members and stakeholders.

If you're interested in becoming a leader, start by observing others and gradually taking on more responsibility. The best way to learn is by doing.

THE FUNDAMENTALS OF LEADERSHIP AND SOFT SKILLS

When it comes to leadership, there are three fundamental principles of what a leader must embody. These three fundamentals ensure that any person who aspires to be a successful leader will succeed by following them. These norms do not change regardless of whether you are in high school or university, working at an office full time, starting your own business, or managing employees, directly and indirectly. So, these should always be kept in the forefront of your mind:

Achievement: Leaders need to achieve results and get things done. They must have a clear vision for the future, set goals, and motivate people to work together towards common objectives.

Relationships: Leaders must build positive relationships with others to create trust, collaborate effectively, and communicate efficiently.

Ethics: Leaders must act with integrity and make moral decisions rather than selfish or driven by personal gain.

So, while the ability to lead might not be innate, it can be learned by following these three fundamentals, which provide a strong foundation for leaders to develop their skills over time. In addition, other soft skills are essential for success, such as communication, problem-solving, and decision-making.

CHAPTER 2

Different Leadership Styles

VARIOUS leadership styles can be employed to achieve success. Some common leadership styles are discussed below. Each style has its own set of pros and cons, and it is essential to select the right style for the situation at hand.

AUTOCRATIC LEADERSHIP

An authoritarian leadership style, also known as dictatorial leadership, is one in which leaders have complete control over all decisions and receive little input from group members. Authoritative leaders typically make judgments and choices based on their ideas and perceptions, rarely accepting suggestions from followers. Autocratic leadership entails absolute authority over a group.

Like other leadership styles, the autocratic style has both its advantages and drawbacks. While those who highly rely on this method are frequently criticized as bossy or dictatorial, it may be beneficial in certain circumstances.

When and where the authoritarian leadership style is most valuable may be determined by various factors, including the situation, the type of work the group is performing, and team member attributes. If you usually employ this kind of leadership in a group setting, studying your approach further as well as the situations in which it works best can be beneficial.

Characteristics of Autocratic Leadership

- The leader makes all decisions unilaterally
- Little input from group members is accepted
- Leader relies heavily on their own ideas and perceptions
- Focuses on goals rather than people
- Provides no rewards or incentives for group members
- Little communication between leader and followers

In some instances, the authoritarian leadership style is a practical choice. It may be instrumental in crises that require quick decision-making with input from team members. In most cases, however, this kind of approach will not achieve optimal results, such as when it is applied to a typical business setting where more input from others would be helpful because it prevents employees who understand their job and roles from contributing ideas on how best to carry out tasks at hand. The autocratic leadership method may work best in short-term projects, such as during times of fast growth or turnaround efforts; leaders may need to make decisions quickly without staff buy-in if they are going to keep up with demand or improve the company's performance.

On the other hand, autocratic leadership can negatively affect team morale and productivity. When followers feel that their input is not valued or respected, they may become discouraged and less motivated to do their best work. Additionally, if there is no communication between leader and followers, misunderstandings may occur, leading to conflict. This leadership style should be used sparingly to avoid these potential issues.

Leaders need to consider all options before implementing an autocratic leadership style. Although it may benefit certain situations, it is not always the best approach for a group working towards common goals. Leaders who are new to this type of management should experiment with different methods to determine which system is most effective in achieving the objectives of a particular project.

Benefits of Autocratic Leadership

The authoritative approach has a stern ring to it. It can be damaging when applied excessively or to the wrong groups or circumstances. In certain situations, such as when decisions must be made fast without consulting many individuals, authoritarian leadership might be advantageous.

Strong leadership is sometimes required for projects in order to get things done quickly and effectively. When the group's most knowledgeable person is authoritarian, rapid, and efficient decisions are more likely to be made. The autocratic leadership style may be beneficial for the following reasons and in the following situations:

Provides Direction: In small groups, authoritarian leadership may work. Have you ever been a part of a team where poor management, a lack of leadership, and a failure to set deadlines caused the project to go off track?

If you are in this situation, your grade or job performance is likely to have suffered as a result. A strong leader that employs an autocratic approach can take control of the group, distribute tasks to various individuals, and set firm deadlines for projects to be completed if this is so.

One of the essential aspects of successful group projects is having one person take responsibility for either leading or simply handling the task independently. The group is more likely to finish the project on time, and see everyone providing equal input, if roles, activities, and deadlines are established.

Relieves Pressure: The autocratic leadership style can end the lack of progress and frustration that a group may feel when trying to complete a task. If no one knows what they are supposed to be doing, or if someone is unsure how they fit into the project as a whole, it's easy for stress levels to rise. When there's confusion about roles or tasks in an unstructured team setting, things often go downhill fast.

A leader who takes control by making decisions and assigning activities will relieve pressure from other members because they interpret information clearly through sound judgment based on proven experience rather than simply assuming specific responsibilities without sufficient input from others. The authoritative approach allows for more productive work sessions where people know their roles and are not afraid to voice their opinions.

A leader can use authoritarian leadership when tasks are not assigned to an individual, or the group is too large for democratic leadership. If you are in charge of a team that needs to get things done before the end of theday, this style may be advantageous because it allows for swift decision- making without having everyone's input first. If mistakes do occur, they will happen quickly and efficiently so that others do not have muchtime to dwell on them – and hopefully learn from what went wrongwhile working towards correcting problems more effectively in future endeavours.

Drawbacks of Autocratic Leadership

Authoritarian leaders often feel pressure since they make final decisions with little support from co-workers who might otherwise provide good ideas or alternative perspectives. This type of leader also does not typically solicit feedback from team members, so they might not be aware of potential problems until it's too late.

In addition, autocratic leadership can breed resentment if team members feel that their ideas are being ignored or are not given a chance to contribute. If this often happens enough, employees may begin to feel unmotivated and will eventually stop putting in the extra effort required for success.

Finally, some people simply do not work well under an authoritarian approach; these individuals tend to perform better when they have more control over their tasks and are not micromanaged constantly by someone else.

LAISSEZ-FAIRE LEADERSHIP

Delegative leadership, also known as hands-off or laissez-faire leadership, is a style of management in which leaders are hands-off and allow team members to make the decisions. Researchers have discovered that this is generally the least productive form of group member productivity.

Laissez-faire leadership may be both beneficial and hazardous. There are also certain circumstances and contexts where laissez-faire leadership is appropriate.

Leaders can check in on staff performance and provide regular feedback to help make laissez-faire leadership more successful. It is also beneficial for executives to determine when this approach works best.

Characteristics of Laissez-faire Leadership

The following are some of the characteristics of laissez-faire leadership:
- Allows team members to make their own decisions
- Gives employees freedom and independence
- Provides little or no direction or instruction
- Offers minimal feedback or supervision
- Has a hands-off approach

Examples of Laissez-faire Leadership

Here's how laissez-faire leadership may appear in various scenarios:

In school: A teacher who gives students the freedom to learn independently and make their own decisions.

At work: A boss who allows employees to develop their own ideas and solutions.

In a relationship: A hands-off partner and does not give a lot of direction or feedback.

Benefits of Laissez-faire Leadership

The laissez-faire style, like other types of leadership, has benefits:

It encourages personal growth: When employees are given the freedom to make their own decisions, they learn and grow as individuals.

It develops problem-solving skills: When employees can form their own solutions, they develop problem-solving skills.

It builds trust: By trusting employees to make decisions on their own, leaders show that they trust them. This can help build stronger relationships.

It encourages creativity and innovation: Laissez-faire leadership allows for new ideas and creativity to flourish.

It allows for faster decision-making: When leaders are not involved in every decision, the process of making decisions is sped up.

Disadvantages of Laissez-faire Leadership

Because the laissez-faire method relies on the team's abilities, it will not work in places where team members lack experience or the skills necessary to complete projects and make informed judgments. This can result in poor job performance and lower job satisfaction.

The following are some of the drawbacks of a laissez-faire approach:

Lack of clarity regarding roles: Employees may not know what is expected of them or how the team functions.

Poor communication: Team members will be less likely to communicate with each other if they make their own decisions and develop individual solutions.

Fewer opportunities for mistakes: When leaders are not involved in all aspects of decision-making, employees have fewer chances to learn from past mistakes that can help them improve performance next time around.

Lack of accountability for results: When no one else is responsible for deciding on outcomes (except perhaps a manager), it is difficult to hold people accountable when things go wrong – which ultimately means poor job performance because there is not enough feedback and guidance, especially when it comes to problem areas where an employee might benefit from some coaching by a manager.

The poor perception among employees: A laissez-faire leadership style does not always create the best impression with employees, who may feel that they are being ignored or left out of decisions concerning critical aspects of their jobs.

Low accountability: When no one is responsible for making decisions or solving problems, it is difficult to hold people accountable when things go wrong, and there isn't enough feedback.

Low commitment: When employees aren't committed to the goals of a laissez-faire leadership style, they may not work as hard since they are not fully invested in their jobs.

Inconsistent performance: A laissez-faire approach can result in inconsistent performances among team members because some will likely outperform others due to differences in skill levels and experience.

Passivity: When leaders aren't involved in solving problems and making decisions, they may come across as passive.

Strengths of Laissez-faire Leaders

If you take a more hands-off approach to leadership, there are times and circumstances where you may perform better. They are as follows:

In creative fields: This style is likely to produce good outcomes when you work in a creative industry where people are highly driven, skilled, inventive, and dedicated to their job.

When working with self-managed teams: This style is also likely to work well if you are working with self-managed teams who always have a plan.

When the people in your team already feel motivated: If they believe that their work environment and leaders care about them (show empathy), it will be easy for them to trust the leadership of others without being micromanaged.

When there is a high employee turnover rate: This strategy works best when employees change jobs frequently or aren't committed long term; those who stay may not need detailed instructions on how tasks should be completed since most of these former workers came from other companies where things were done differently anyway.

When you can afford staff losses/turnover: When key positions must be filled quickly due to frequent departures by employees, you may want to rely on a laissez-faire approach for the time being.

When your team members are highly experienced: If they have been in their positions long enough and know how things should be done, which minimizes management's involvement, this style is likely to work best.

When it doesn't affect customer satisfaction or employee commitment: Since many of these workers will already feel motivated by an effective leader who cares about them (empathy), a lack of guidance might not cause problems when customers haven't been affected or if their job performance isn't always consistent from one person to another since there is no need to provide detailed instructions on precisely what needs to be done each day — especially if employee turnover rate is high as described above. If employees are not fully committed to the goals of a laissez-faire leadership style, they may not work as hard since they are not fully invested in their jobs.

AUTHORITATIVE LEADERSHIP

Authoritative leadership is a type of leadership where the leader has power and uses it to get things done. Authoritative leaders are often decisive and can make quick decisions when needed. They are also good at getting their team on board with their vision and motivating them to achieve common goals. However, they can also be demanding and expect a lot from their team.

If you're looking for a leader who can get things done quickly and efficiently, an authoritative leader may be right for you. Just understand what this type of leader expects from their team members before signing up!

Characteristics of Authoritative Leadership

The following are some of the characteristics of authoritative leaders:

- Decisive
- Makes quick decisions when needed
- Can get a team on board with a certain vision
- Motivating
- Demanding
- Expects a lot from team members

Benefits of Authoritative Leadership

There are several benefits of authoritative leadership, including:

Decisive action: Authoritative leaders make quick decisions when needed, which can be helpful in a crisis.

Goal alignment: Authoritative leaders create a vision that their team can get behind and this allows them to achieve common goals. This can lead to increased productivity and motivation.

Efficient operation: Authoritative leaders often have a clear idea of what they want to achieve and how to do it. This leads to more efficient operations, saving time and money.

Discipline: Authoritative leaders often set clear expectations for their teams and require them to meet those goals, providing a sense of order that helps team members feel more motivated when they know what is expected of them.

Disadvantages of Authoritative Leadership

There are also a few disadvantages of authoritative leadership, including:

Dictatorial style: While there are some benefits to having clear expectations and goals, leaders who set too many rules without explaining them can be seen as dictatorial. This makes it harder for team members to get on board with their vision or feel motivated to achieve common goals.

Intolerance of failure: Authoritative leaders often have high standards that they want to be met by their teams, so those who fail at meeting these standards may not remain in the leader's good books for very long. Those who do not meet performance benchmarks need extra encouragement to perform well again – if they ever do! Leaders may choose to find new people who are more qualified to fill empty positions rather than helping underperforming team members improve.

Difficult to work for: While most leaders who are willing to be authoritative have a clear vision that they are trying to achieve, some can also come off as demanding and difficult to please. This may lead to their teams feeling demoralized or unappreciated, moving them toward disengagement rather than the motivation to avoid not meeting the leader's standards again!

Will not provide more resources when needed: Authoritative leaders often prefer efficient operations over having all of the necessary tools and staff on hand. They tend not to want an abundance of overhead costs because they feel it will slow down progress towards their goals; however, this means that if any additional resources become necessary, you'll need someone else (like your boss) to help provide them.

May create a divide between leader and team: Authoritative leadership is often associated with stereotypes of strict military leaders or CEOs who are focused on efficiency over all else, including their team's happiness. This can lead to resentment among the team towards the leader and make it harder for members to get behind their vision. It may also cause less experienced staff (i.e., newer hires) to feel intimidated by senior staffers because they have more experience in executing the leader's demands effectively while new employees will struggle under those same demands!

PACESETTING LEADERSHIP

One of the most important qualities of leadership is being able to set and maintain a high standard. Pacesetting leaders are constantly raising the bar, pushing themselves to improve their own skills and performance. They do not just demand excellence from those around them but also themselves. This sets an example for others and inspires them to reach higher levels of success.

Pacesetting leaders often have a strong sense of personal accountability, taking responsibility for their actions and mistakes. They look at what they can do to correct the situation themselves and do not make excuses or blame others. This level of integrity builds trust and respect among followers.

Pacesetting leaders typically have a clear vision and purpose, which they can articulate in a way that inspires others. They can develop and articulate a strategy and then execute it effectively. This combination of vision and execution makes pacesetting leaders stand out from the pack.

If you want to become a pacesetting leader, start by setting high standards for yourself and always striving to improve. Be honest and accountable, have a clear vision and purpose, and be an influential strategist and executor.

Characteristics of Pacesetting Leadership

A pacesetting leader has several characteristics that set them apart from others. It is essential to know and develop these qualities to improve your leadership skills.

See if any of the following sound familiar:

- **Constantly setting new goals for myself**: I tend to push forward without looking back because results get me excited! By continually raising my standards, I can accomplish more than anyone else around me. When something is easy for me, it becomes boring; therefore, I seek out challenges as opportunities for growth and improvement instead of making excuses to not do anything. I think that every day should be better than the last on all fronts (professional, physical, emotional, etc.), if possible.

- **A personal sense of accountability**: I take ownership of my successes and failures. If things go wrong, I did something wrong, not because someone else dropped the ball. This mindset builds trust and respect within teams I work in as people know that they can count on me to be truthful and straightforward at all times.

- **Clear vision and purpose**: From the time I wake up in the morning until I fall asleep at night, everything that I do should have a specific goal or outcome in mind. Whether it's developing new skills/knowledge or making an impact on others, there needs to be a north star to guide my decisions and actions. Without this level of focus, it's too easy for me to get side-tracked and lose sight of the big picture.

- **Excellent communication skills**: I tend to talk fast (incredibly excited), but that doesn't mean my message isn't clear. I take the time to listen carefully before responding to ensure everyone is on the same page. In addition, I always communicate with others in a respectful and considerate way regardless of their rank or position within the company.

Benefits of Pacesetting Leadership

Pacesetting leadership has many benefits for both the leader and their followers. The most significant ones are:

- **Inspires a high-performance culture**: People want to be involved with organizations that produce results, which is why pacesetting leaders often attract top talent who want to work on their exciting projects/initiatives. When they see how well things are run under this type of leader, others naturally get excited about being part of things as well (and will likely follow in their footsteps).

- **Increases productivity and efficiency**: By defining clear expectations of people at all levels within an organization (including yourself), you can ensure everyone knows what needs to happen before making any decisions or taking action. This ensures nothing gets done twice and that there is no wasted time or effort on the part of your team.

- **Generates employee engagement**: When people clearly understand what is required to achieve goals, they are more likely to be engaged in their work/role as they know how it contributes to overall company success. This type of leader also creates an environment where employees feel comfortable being themselves (instead of putting on a front), which further encourages high performance among followers instead of putting unnecessary pressure on them. As pacesetting leaders are not afraid to encourage one another when things go well, this spreads positive energy throughout the organization, boosting morale and productivity!

Disadvantages of Pacesetting Leadership

While there are many advantages to being a pacesetting leader, there are also some potential disadvantages that should be considered:

- **Can be demanding/stressful**: This type of leadership style often puts a lot of pressure on the individual to produce constant results. If not managed correctly, this can lead to high-stress levels and burnout over time.

- **Requires significant knowledge and experience**: Pacesetting leaders need an in-depth understanding of what they are doing to set the right example for their followers. Without this level of expertise, it can be difficult (if not impossible) to maintain control over the overall direction and progress of the organization.

- **May alienate people**: This type of leadership can be perceived as demanding, inflexible, and unapproachable, resulting in team members feeling isolated or left out. While this is not always the case, it's something to be aware of if you decide to take on this role.

- In conclusion, pacesetting leadership is a great way to inspire high performance within an organization while maintaining control over progress and direction. However, it is essential to be aware of the potential disadvantages of this leadership style to make sure it does not hurt your team.

DEMOCRATIC LEADERSHIP

Democratic leadership is a style of leadership that focuses on the collective good rather than individual achievement. This type of leadership often relies on collaboration and consultation with team members in order to make decisions. Democratic leaders believe that by engaging with team members and considering their opinions, they can create a more effective team overall.

One of the fundamental principles of democratic leadership is trust. A democratic leader must trust their team to participate in decision-making. They must also be willing to listen to input from all members of the group, even those who do not traditionally have a say in such matters. This type of leader values the diversity of opinion and believes it leads to better decision-making.

Democratic leadership can be complex because it requires a certain amount of trust. If team members do not believe that their leader is open to new ideas and willing to consider all possible solutions, they may feel less motivated to contribute. Democratic leadership will also fail if the democratic leader does not adequately consult with their team; simply asking for input without listening carefully can leave team members feeling ignored rather than empowered by the process.

Characteristics of Democratic Leadership

Democratic leadership is similar to transformational leadership in that both styles require their leaders to be strong and charismatic figures. Democratic leaders are also concerned with the growth of their team members and believe that self-leadership requires responsibility for one's actions.

Benefits of Democratic Leadership

Democratic leadership has several benefits, the most important of which is the creation of a more effective team. By involving team members in the decision-making process, democratic leaders can form a more motivated and productive team. In addition, teams that use democratic leadership are often better at problem-solving because they have access to a broaderrange of ideas.

Democratic leadership also promotes trust and respect within teams. When team members feel that their voices are heard and that they have control in their work environment, they are likely to be more committed to their team's success. Finally, democratic leadership helps build relationships between team members. When people feel like they are part of a group working towards a common goal, they are more likely to cooperate and get along.

CHAPTER 3

How to Become a Leader

To become a leader, you have to start by learning the basics. Leadership is not about being in charge or telling people what to do. It is about making things happen and inspiring others to achieve great things.

One of the essential traits for a leader is determination. Leaders need to stick to their goals and push through any obstacles in their way. They also need to motivate others and make them work towards common goals. A good leader knows how to take charge, but they are also willing to listen and learn from those around them.

There are many ways that you can develop your leadership skills. One of the best ways is by reading books on leadership or attending workshops or seminars on the topic. You can also watch videos or listen to podcasts about leadership and its qualities. There are many resources available online and in print form.

Another great way to develop your leadership skills is by practicing them regularly. Try leading a team project at work or volunteering to head up a committee or event. Take on new challenges and tasks that will allow you to develop your skills.

Leadership is not something that comes naturally to everyone, but it can be learned. It takes time, effort, and practice, but the rewards are worth it. When you become a leader, you can make a difference in the world and help others achieve their goals.

Here are some tips on how to become a leader:

Start by developing your skill set: Become an expert in your field and learn everything you can about leadership. Study different techniques and strategies, and find out what works best for you.

Build relationships: Leaders can inspire others because they have strong relationships with them. Get to know the people you work with and develop trust and mutual respect.

Be authentic: People want to follow someone genuine and honest. Do not try to be something you're not – just be yourself and let your true personality shine through.

Stay positive: Leaders are optimistic, forward-thinking individuals who always see the best in people and situations. Keep a positive attitude even when things go wrong.

Be respectful: One of the most important leadership qualities is respect; if you do not have it from your employees or colleagues, you won't lead them effectively. Showing others that you appreciate their contributions will make all the difference!

Treat everyone equally: Everyone deserves equal opportunity, regardless of their race or social status. Treating everyone the same will help build a sense of community and belonging among your team members.

Work hard: Show that you are willing to put in more effort than anyone else by working through problems until they are solved – no matter how long it takes!

Learn from mistakes: Do not be afraid to make mistakes; everybody makes them sometimes, even leaders like you. Learn from your mistakes and move on so they do not happen again in the future!

Be true to yourself: Don't try to emulate others or do things that go against your values because of peer pressure – everyone will respect you more if you are honest about who you are.

Embrace change: Leaders know that change is inevitable and welcome it instead of fearing it. Be prepared to adapt when changes occur in your workplace or personal life.

Make a difference: Leaders are always looking for ways to improve things, whether their team's productivity or the world around them. What can you do to make a positive impact in your community?

CHAPTER 4

Leading Teams and Groups

WORKING in teams and groups is necessary to be a good employee, manager, or leader. When you are leading others, it can be tough to achieve great results without the team pulling together and working towards common goals that suit everyone's needs.

Here we will look at some of these skills needed when managing a group work project:

You need to set clear expectations of what you expect from your co-workers, both individually and collectively. It may also mean having people who do not want to follow specific rules leave your team, so they do not drag down those who care about doing what is suitable for this collaborative process. This does not mean forcing anyone out but instead having an open discussion and politely parting ways if they are not a good fit.

You need to communicate effectively with your team members. This means both listening to them and conveying the messages you want to be delivered in a way that they will understand. This also includes body language, which can often communicate more than words.

Be aware of different working styles and how people like to work. Some people are early birds, while others may prefer getting down to business after lunch; try and plan around these natural tendencies, when possible, rather than trying to change them.

Be patient with your team and give everyone time to adjust, learn and grow into their new roles. Remember that everyone makes mistakes, so do not be too hard on them; instead, try and give them space to learn from their mistakes.

Leadership skills are necessary for group work projects. They help everyone involved achieve the desired results without wasting time or effort because somebody was not doing what was expected of them.

CHAPTER 5

Motivating Employees and Team Members

EMPLOYEES and team members come to work for many different reasons. While some may be in it because they want to, others just need a pay check or have no other choice. Regardless of why they are there, you can motivate employees and team members into being more productive by following the tips below:

Understand what motivates them: Everyone is different, and what motivates one person may not motivate another. Take the time to understand what drives your employees or team members and use that information to encourage them.

Encourage them: When someone does a good job, tell them! Praise their efforts and let them know you appreciate their work. This will encourage them to continue working hard.

Create a positive work environment: A hostile work environment can be very demotivating, so do everything you can to create a positive one. This includes having clear expectations, providing constructive feedback, and maintaining an open line of communication.

Offer incentives: Sometimes giving employees or team members something they want will motivate them. If you know your employees or team members are motivated by free food, time off, and other such rewards, then make sure they get them!

Be a good leader: Employees look up to their leaders – if you are doing a great job as the group leader, this can serve as an example for others who may not have been following suit. You should also take care of your employees to show that you care about them. Whether it is something simple like paying for lunch or more significant gestures like mentoring someone at work who needs help with their career path, there are several things you can do to show that you care.

Take a break! Employees who work all day without taking any time off may become demotivated, so they must take breaks throughout the day to maintain their energy levels. These breaks should be relatively short – each employee is different, but most people need at least 15 minutes of rest after every hour or two of intense activity.

HANDLING CONFLICT IN THE WORKPLACE

Conflict is a natural and inevitable part of any workplace. It can arise from different personalities, work styles, or simply different opinions on how something should be done. However, when conflict is not handled correctly, it can lead to tension, stress, and decreased productivity.

Handling conflict in the workplace can be one of the most challenging things. You must handle any dispute professionally so as not to affect your work.

There are several things that you can do to handle conflict in the workplace effectively:

Address the issue head-on. Do not try to ignore or avoid the problem. Address it directly and honestly with all involved parties, and be open to listening to their concerns as well.

Stay calm and professional. Avoid getting emotional or personal during the dispute. Stay focused on finding a resolution.

Be willing to compromise. No one will get everything they want in a conflict situation, so be ready to compromise in order to find a resolution.

Keep communication open. Ensure that everyone involved in the conflict is kept up to date on what is happening and how the situation progresses. This will help avoid any misunderstandings.

You can handle workplace conflict effectively and hopefully resolve it without damaging relationships or productivity by following these above tips.

CHAPTER 6

Leadership Style

THE first step to self-leadership is clearly understanding what leadership means and how you can define it for yourself. When we think of great leaders, our minds often go towards people who are charismatic or who possess an exceptional ability to lead others effectively. With that mindset alone, one could easily conclude that they do not have enough charisma or whatever else is deemed necessary by society as a whole to be able to become influential leaders themselves.

But this mentality is wrong and will only hold you back from unlocking your full potential when successfully leading others! The truth about being an effective leader lies within the philosophy behind why an individual has chosen such a role in the first place. There are many different types of leaders. Each can be successful if they stick to what works best for them, rather than trying to emulate someone else's style or following somebody else's playbook without fully understanding it.

Having a deep understanding of yourself and what you wish to achieve is the first step to becoming an effective leader. Once this has been accomplished, it is all about acting on your terms based on how you want things done instead of being influenced by external factors such as peer pressure.

CHOOSING YOUR STYLE

Being a good leader entails knowing which leadership style is best for you. Developing a distinct style and expanding into others as needed may help you be a more effective leader. Start by following these steps:

Know yourself: Begin by determining your current dominant leadership style. Ask respected co-workers to describe the benefits of your leadership approach. You might also take a leadership style assessment to discover more about yourself.

Draw upon your strengths: Capitalize on your natural strengths once you know which style works best for you. For example, if you are task-oriented, focus on getting the job done and setting measurable goals. However, if people are drawn to your personality or vision, emphasize those qualities when leading others.

Be flexible: Although it is important to be true to yourself, understand that there will be times when adjustments are necessary. A good leader can adapt to different situations without compromising their values.

Understand the different styles: Familiarize yourself with the various leadership styles available. What new abilities do you need to improve your skills?

Practice: Make sure you are authentic with every approach you take. It might be challenging to change your leadership style from one to the other. Continue practicing the new behaviours until they become natural. In other words, do not let go of who you are.

Stay agile: A good leader is flexible and willing to change when necessary. However, that does not mean being wishy-washy; you should have a plan and stick with it until the end unless there is a compelling reason not to do so – one that could improve your chances of success.

LEADERSHIP STYLES

There are many leadership styles that one could choose from to become an effective leader; below, we will go over some of the more popular ones to get a better understanding of what they entail and how to choose the best one for yourself.

Task-oriented (Doer): This type of leader is all about getting things done when it comes down to business instead of focusing on interpersonal relationships and other non-business matters that may not be a part of their job description. These types can lead by example because they tend to go out into the trenches with everyone else to get essential tasks completed; this helps them gain respect from others who appreciate someone who takes action and doesn't talk too much or mince words instead of being productive! This leadership style works well for people whose goal is complete productivity rather than increasing morale within an organizationdue to its focus on work rather than the people.

Relationship-oriented (People Person): This type of leader is all about maintaining an environment where everyone gets along, feels connected, and is inspired to do their best because they are passionate about doing! The leaders who follow this style often have extensive interpersonal skills that help them connect with almost any individual, regardless of whether it is within a business or outside of it. They tend to focus on building trusting relationships as well as fostering a sense of positive teamwork among those around them; this gives others the feeling that "we" can accomplish anything together rather than just focusing on individuals working alone, which builds morale and makes employees feel good about themselves, thus producing better results due to workers enjoying themselves while working.

Visionary (Big Picture): This type of leader has a clear vision for what they want their team to achieve and can articulate it in a way that inspires others to buy into the idea and help make it happen! They often come up with new ideas, think outside the box, and present creative solutions, which can benefit any company or organization. However, these leaders can sometimes struggle when it comes down to details and may need someone else who is more task-oriented on their team to help them see things through; this is because they tend to focus on the end goal rather than all of the little steps that are necessary to get there.

Command-and-Control (Authoritative): This type of leader is what most people think of when they hear the word "leader." They are often decisive, have a clear vision, and like to be in control. But making quick decisions without always considering everyone else's opinion can sometimes result in conflict. This style can work well, however, if a team is already familiar with what needs to get done and does not require much guidance or hand-holding from the leader. On the other hand, this approach can also lead to employees feeling unappreciated or micromanaged if used too frequently, resulting in less motivation and more stress.

Coaching/Empowering (Nurturing): This type of leader takes a more hands-off approach and focuses on coaching their team members to be the best they can be. They provide support, feedback, and guidance when necessary but ultimately want employees to feel autonomous and in control of their work, resulting in more investment from their team. This style often works well with teams that are newer or have less experience since the leader can spend more time training them and developing their skills; however, it may not be as effective with teams who are already familiar with what needs to get done or those who require more direction from a leader.

Now that you understand some of the different leadership styles, how do you decide which one is right for you? Most people fall somewhere in between two or a few of these styles, and at the end of the day, it just comes down to what works best for you; however, some people may be more inclined towards a particular style due to their personality.

CHAPTER 7

What is Management?

M ANAGEMENT is the process of planning, organizing, leading, and controlling an organization's resources to achieve its goals. Management includes setting objectives, allocating resources, designing structures and processes, motivating and communicating with people, and assessing results. In other words, it's everything that goes into making sure an organization runs smoothly.

While there are many different theories and models of management, all managers share some common goals: to ensure their organization operates effectively and efficiently, meets its objectives, and provides a good return on investment for its stakeholders.

Successful managers employ several critical skills to carry out these duties effectively. These skills include leadership, problem-solving, decision-making, communication, team-building, and change management.

LEADING VS. MANAGING

Management and leadership are often used interchangeably, but they have distinct definitions. Management refers to the planning of resources to achieve organizational goals. On the other hand, a leader motivates individuals towards achieving common objectives by leading them through inspiration and creating a shared vision for their success. The management role involves monitoring progress against deadlines, preparing reports, controlling costs and quality standards. In contrast, leaders inspire others to think about opportunities differently in order to make better decisions regarding sharing knowledge between teams or departments alike.

WHAT IS THE DIFFERENCE BETWEEN LEADERSHIP AND MANAGEMENT?

Process vs. Vision

A vision for change lies at the heart of effective leadership. Managers are primarily interested in implementing procedures like budgeting, organizational structure, and hiring to fulfil company objectives. On the other hand, leaders are more concerned with anticipating events and seizing chances. They can take risks and accept failure as a means to achieving success. Leaders focus on starting something new, while managers seek ways of improving what already exists.

Organizing vs. Aligning

Managers are task-oriented. They focus on getting things done through others. Leaders, in contrast, concentrate more of their time and energy on communicating a vision for change that inspires and motivates individuals to be committed to the organization's goals.

Position vs. Quality

Managers decide what is to be done, how and by whom. Leaders ask questions like: "Why are we doing this?" or "What does the future hold for us? How can I motivate others towards achieving our goals?".

Leaders initiate change; managers maintain order. While a manager focuses on getting things done through people in an established hierarchy (chain of command), leaders seek ways of building a form of teamwork that enhances cross-functional collaboration. A leader encourages individuals to work together as one unit toward common objectives. At the same time, a manager divides responsibilities between teams and departments based upon assigned roles and tasks that must be completed to meet deadlines/ goals set forth by each team supervisor. Managers tend to have more staff experience than leaders, who often come from the ranks of executives.

Leading people vs. Managing work

Manager's focus is on getting work done through others. A leader aims to get the best out of people, developing their potential and supporting them to achieve greatness together. Leaders are concerned with people and how they work together. Managers, in contrast, concentrate more of their time and energy communicating a vision for change that inspires individuals to be committed to achieving an organization's goals.

CHAPTER 8

The Attributes of a Leader

A good leader is someone who can motivate and inspire people. They have a clear vision and can communicate it effectively. They are also decisive and can make tough decisions when needed. They also can build relationships and trust with others.

Many different leadership styles share common attributes, but a good leader must be motivated and able to inspire others, have a clear vision, be decisive, want to build relationships and trust, and be adaptable. Leaders come in all shapes and sizes, so there is no perfect way to lead. What works for one person may not work for another. The important thing is that you find what works best for you and stick to it.

Leadership is not just for managers or executives. Anyone can be a leader, regardless of their position in the company. It is essential to develop your leadership skills to take control of your career and future.

DEALING WITH CHANGE

Change is inevitable. Sometimes it is for the better, and sometimes not so much. Whether you are experiencing change because of a promotion or new job opportunity, or if your company has decided to make some changes that affect operations in your department, change can be challenging to handle at first. It may seem like everything will fall apart without warning, and there are no rules about how to deal with this sudden change; however, the truth is that most people have already dealt with numerous situations similar to yours before. So, relax! You have come through tough times back, and you will do it again now.

Conflict Resolution

Conflict is a normal and natural part of life. It can arise in personal relationships, work, or other situations where people interact. The key to resolving conflicts effectively is communication. You need to listen to the other person's point of view and understand their perspective. Once you have done that, it is time to compromise. Each side needs to give a little bit so that everyone can feel like they have won something. Finally, do not forget to apologize if necessary. Apologizing shows that you take responsibility for your actions and value the relationship more than winning an argument.

Building Trust and Respect

Trust and respect are both important, but they are not the same thing. To have a trusting relationship with someone else, you need to be able to count on them in difficult situations. They also need to be consistent in their behaviour and keep their promises. On the other hand, respect is more about how others see you as an individual; it is not necessarily tied to a specific situation or timeframe. For example, if your family sees you as respectable because you have many great qualities that they admire, then this trust will extend itself throughout all areas of life for them.

Delegation

One of the keys to becoming a successful leader is delegation. This means that you need to trust your subordinates to do their jobs without micromanaging them. This can be difficult at first, but it is essential to let go and allow people to make their own decisions. You may need to provide guidance and feedback, but ultimately, the decision should be theirs. By delegating tasks, you will free up time for yourself to focus on more important things, such as strategy and long-term planning.

Emotional Intelligence

Leaders need to understand their own emotions and the emotions of others. This is known as emotional intelligence or EQ. When you have high EQ, you are able to control your emotions, respond effectively to stressful situations, and build relationships with other people. Emotionally intelligent leaders are more successful than those who are not. They are better at problem-solving, decision-making, and networking.

Many people think that EQ is the same as IQ, but it is very different. While IQ relates to intelligence and logic skills, EQ has more to do with interpersonal relationships. Most experts agree that successful leaders need both high emotional intelligence and strong analytical and problem-solving skills to succeed at their jobs

Collaboration And Teamwork

To be successful, leaders need to work well with others. This means effective collaboration and teamwork. When people work together, they can achieve more than they could individually. They can share resources, ideas, and expertise. The best teams are those in which everyone feels like they are welcome and that their contributions are valued.

Ethics And Integrity

An ethical leader treats others with respect, honesty, and fairness. When you have strong ethics, your work reflects the values of those around you. This makes people trust you because they know what to expect from you in a situation. People also appreciate being treated fairly and not having their time or energy wasted by being misdirected on useless tasks or activities.

Critical Thinking

Critical thinking is the ability to analyse information and come up with solutions. It helps you think about things from different angles so that your decisions are based on evidence rather than feelings or past experiences. You need critical thinking skills to make changes happen, solve problems, and find new opportunities for growth and success at work

Risk Assessment and Risk-based Decisions

Leaders need to be able to make risk-based decisions. This means that they need to weigh the risks and benefits of a particular course of action before deciding on one. They also need to be aware of the potential consequences of their choices, both good and bad. Leaders can achieve great things by taking risks, but they also need to be prepared for when things go wrong.

Research Skills

Research skills are essential for all leaders. This means that you need to be able to gather information effectively and make informed decisions. The most effective leaders do research regularly so they can solve problems, plan strategies, and achieve goals efficiently.

Report Writing

Report writing is another essential skill for leaders. When you write reports, you can share information with others clearly and concisely. This helps ensure that everyone understands what is happening and why decisions are being made. Good report writers also use data to back up their claims so that readers can see the evidence for themselves.

Communication Skills

Leaders need to be able to communicate effectively with others. This means being able to express your ideas clearly and convincingly, as well as listening carefully to what other people have to say. Leaders who can communicate well are more successful than those who cannot. They are better at networking, problem-solving, and decision-making. To be a good communicator, you need to be patient and understand that not everyone thinks in the same way that you do. It will help if you are also willing to compromise and consider other people's opinions on occasion.

Presentation Skills

Leaders need to be able to give good presentations. This means being well prepared, using visual aids, and communicating clearly with their audience. Good leaders are confident speakers who can hold people's attention while they are speaking and make a lasting impression on listeners after the presentation is finished.

Career Planning

Leaders also need to be good at career planning. This means setting goals and creating a plan of action to help them achieve those goals. It is essential to have a clear idea of what you want from your career and what steps you need to take to get there. Career planning skills can help you move up the ladder at work or change careers altogether if you decide it is best for you.

Continuous Learning

Finally, leaders need to be able to keep learning. This means seeking out new information about your industry and staying up-to-date with the latest research so that you do not fall behind in your field. It also means being open to feedback from others and recognizing when it is time for a change or an improvement. Being willing to learn is one of the best qualities that any leader can have.

The skills listed above are just a few of the many soft skills that leaders need to succeed. By developing these skills, you will be able to lead yourself and others better. Soft skills can be learned and improved upon over time, so do not feel discouraged if you are not good at them yet. You will get better at them and become an even more effective leader with practice.

Conclusion

As a leader, you are responsible for motivating your team to be the best they can be as well as handling any conflict that arises. One way of doing this is by understanding what type of leadership style works best with each individual on your team. For instance, some people might respond better to management than leading, while others may need more direction from their managers. A good manager will always consider different personality types so they can get the most out of their employees and team members, ensuring success at both work and home.

In the end, being a good leader starts from within. By setting an example for your team by practicing self-leadership and leading yourself to be successful every day, you'll develop a tone that everyone else on your team will follow. It might take some time, but it pays off significantly in the long run, especially when you form bonds with each team member – they will look up to their manager because they inspire them at work and outside of work, both spiritually and mentally.

This concludes our guide about leadership skills! I hope this information has been helpful for anyone looking into starting in management or already managing others.

CHAPTER 9

The Foundations and Philosophy of Ethical Behaviour

THE financial crime professional's world is one of strict ethics and regulations. It is essential to have a strong understanding of the philosophy behind ethical behaviour to ensure that all actions taken align with the law as well as the organization's values. This section will provide an overview of some of the key concepts involved in ethical thinking.

THE THREE LEVELS OF ETHICS

It is not easy to define clear and acceptable ethics to everyone. However, it may be beneficial to consider the various levels of ethical debate and analysis.

In a specific scenario, we ought to do the most common ethical issue. These inquiries are more basic, at least partially, and focus on such concepts as right and wrong and good and evil more generally. And some moral philosophy discourse is even more abstract.

There are three ethics levels, from the most abstract to the most concrete: metaethics, normative ethics, and applied ethics. It is an excellent first step toward understanding the subject at hand if you know these three levels.

Metaethics

The first level, metaethics, is the most abstract and deals with the origins of ethics and ethical language. It asks questions such as: What is the nature of moral judgments? Are they objective or subjective? Can they be verified empirically?

Metaethics does not offer any answers to these questions but instead considers them further. This level of inquiry is essential to better understand how ethical thought works and determine which concepts are worth exploring in greater depth.

The nature of morality is the subject of metaethics. The following sorts of questions are addressed by metaethics:

- What does it imply when someone claims something is "great" or "correct"?
- What do ethical judgments mean?
- Are they objective or subjective?
- Is it possible to derive an absolute morality from the first principles?
- What is a moral value, and where does it originate?
- Is morality a natural human impulse that we all feel, dependent on individuals or cultures?
- Is it true that moral facts exist?

If you want to know whether a specific action is good or bad, it is best not to look at metaethical questions. However, if you are trying to figure out if a particular behaviour is right or wrong, you'll never get there pondering on them. On the other hand, metaethical queries such as: Why be ethical? or why does the decent thing seem so tricky? are vital for anybody interested in ethics. And they are not easy questions to answer.

Normative Ethics

The second level, normative ethics, deals with ethical theories and moral principles. It asks questions such as: What are the most important moral values? How should these values be applied in specific situations?

Normative ethical theories attempt to provide reasoned answers to these sorts of questions. The three most common types of normative ethical theory are consequentialism, deontology, and virtue ethics.

Virtue Ethics: One of the oldest normative ethical theories is virtue ethics. This approach focuses on developing good traits or virtues, such as honesty, courage, and generosity. Overall, the goal is to be a good person rather than simply following rules or seeking only positive outcomes for yourself.

It is important to note that virtue ethics does not disregard the importance of rules and consequences. However, it emphasizes personal character and believes that a virtuous person will make good decisions, even in difficult situations, because they have a solid moral compass.

Consequentialism: The main idea behind consequentialism is that the morality of an action should be judged by its results. This theory holds that the end justifies the means as long as the future is desirable. In other words, any act, no matter how unethical, is acceptable if it leads to a goodoutcome.

One problem with consequentialism is determining what constitutes a good outcome. What one person might consider beneficial could be seen as disastrous by somebody else. And there is no one correct answer to this question.

Deontology: Deontology focuses on the duty of an action rather than its consequences. This theory holds that specific moral laws must be followed, regardless of the results. Breaking these laws is wrong, even if it leads to a good outcome.

One problem with deontology is that it can be challenging to determine what actions fall under the category of "duty." What might seem like an obvious duty to one person could be considered optional by somebody else. And again, there is no one correct answer to this question.

Applied Ethics

The third level, applied ethics, deals with specific ethical issues and how they should be handled. It asks questions such as: Is it ever okay to lie? Is euthanasia morally acceptable? Should we always obey the law?

Applied ethics considers all of the different normative ethical theories and tries to find a solution to the best moral dilemmas for everyone involved. This can be a difficult task, as conflicting views on handling an issue often prompt discussion and delay.

One example of this is the debate over abortion. Some people believe that abortion is always wrong, no matter the circumstances. Others think that abortions should be allowed in cases of rape or when the mother's life is in danger. There is no one right answer to this question, and people often disagree on which side is correct or ethical.

The study of applied ethics entails examining specific moral issues in public or private life. While normative ethics tries to establish broad norms for morality, applied ethics is concerned with particular moral disputes. Abortion, stem cell research, environmental concerns, and animal treatment are just a few examples of applied ethical quandaries.

Normative ethical theories, principles or rules derived from such theories, or analogical reasoning (which analyses moral issues by comparing them to comparable situations) may all be utilized in applied ethics. Context-specific norms or expectations, such as those that characterize a particular profession (e.g., medicine or journalism), arrangement (e.g., an agreement between two parties), or relationship (e.g., parent-child), are also important when applying ethical analysis.

PHILOSOPHY OF ETHICAL BEHAVIOUR

The philosophy of ethical behaviour is the basis of any sound financial crime professional. You must always act with integrity and in your clients' best interests, no matter the situation or circumstances. This means being honest and transparent in all your dealings, even when it may be difficult or inconvenient for you to do so. It also means refusing to take shortcuts or engaging in unethical behaviour, such as bribery or corruption. By following this philosophy, you can build a reputation as an honest and reliable professional, which will benefit you throughout your career.

In addition to following a philosophy of ethical behaviour, it is crucial to develop a strong understanding of financial crime laws and regulations. This knowledge will help you stay on top of the latest changes in the field and ensure that you are always acting within the law. It is also essential to have strong investigative skills in order to be able to uncover financial crime schemes effectively.

Suppose you want to be successful in the field of financial crime investigation, money laundering prevention, and other related disciplines. In that case, you need to be prepared to work hard and learn as much as possible. However, with the right attitude and skill set, you can make great strides in your career and help protect society from financial criminals.

THE IMPACT OF ETHICS ON SOCIETY

The impact of ethics on society is undeniable. By following a code of ethics, financial crime professionals help maintain the trust and integrity of our economic system. This, in turn, helps ensure that businesses can operate fairly and honestly and that consumers are protected from fraud and other schemes.

Inaddition, byupholdinghighethicalstandards, financialcrimeprofessionals set an example for others to follow. This can help create a culture of honesty and integrity, which is essential for the healthy functioning of any society. Ultimately, the role of financial crime professionals in promoting ethical behaviour is vital to the well-being of our communities and our economy as a whole.

CHAPTER 10

Codes of Conduct and Professionalism

A code of conduct is a set of principles that guides the behaviour of an individual or group. Codes of conduct exist in many different professions, and they often outline the standards of behaviour expected from members of the profession.

Many financial crime associations have codes of conduct. The ACFE, for example, has the Code of Professional Ethics. The code lays out a set of principles that financial crime professionals should follow to maintain the integrity and professionalism of the field. Some key points from the code include:

Honesty and Integrity: Financial crime professionals must always act with honesty and integrity in their professional and personal lives.

Confidentiality: Financial crime professionals must keep all information obtained during their work confidential. This includes not sharing any information about investigations or clients with unauthorized individuals.

Professionalism: Financial crime professionals must always act professionally with clients and other professionals, as well as in their general conduct.

Avoiding Conflicts of Interest: Financial crime professionals must avoid any conflicts of interest that could compromise their ability to do their job correctly.

Acting with integrity: You should always act honestly and ethically, even when making tough decisions.

Not engaging in bribery or corruption: It is essential to maintain the public's trust by refusing to engage in illegal activities.

Abiding by the law: You must comply with all applicable laws and regulations governing financial crime.

By following these codes of conduct, you can help ensure that you are viewed as a reputable and trustworthy member of the financial crime community.

Following these codes of conduct will help you uphold the high standards expected of those in this field. It is also essential to be aware of potential ethical traps that may occur in your work. For example, you may be faced with the decision of whether to report a suspected crime or protect a client. It is crucial to weigh all the factors involved and decide what is best for everyone involved.

Being a responsible and ethical financial crime professional can help ensure that this field remains trustworthy and respected.

WHY ARE CODES OF CONDUCT NECESSARY?

Codes of conduct are essential because they help maintain the integrity and professionalism. They guide members of the profession on acting ethically and responsibly in their work.

When professions have codes of conduct, it helps ensure that everyone involved in that profession behaves responsibly. This can help build trust between professionals and the public. It can also help protect the reputation of the profession as a whole.

If you are considering entering into a career in financial crime, it is essential to be familiar with the code of conduct that applies to that field. By following these guidelines, you can help ensure that you always act with integrity and professionalism. This will reflect positively on you and your chosen profession.

WHAT SHOULD BE INCLUDED IN A CODE OF CONDUCT?

A code of conduct should include a set of principles that members of the profession are expected to follow. These principles should be based on the values and ethics of the profession. They should also be in line with applicable laws and regulations.

When drafting a code of conduct, it is essential to consider all potential ethical traps in a professional's work. For example, you may need to weigh the pros and cons of reporting a suspected crime. It would also help guide how professionals should deal with conflicts of interest.

The code of conduct should be reviewed and updated regularly to reflect the latest changes in law and ethics. It is also essential to communicate the code to all professional members so they know the expectations of them.

HOW CAN CODES OF CONDUCT HELP WITH PROFESSIONAL DEVELOPMENT?

A code of conduct can be a valuable tool for professional development by guiding ethical and legal principles. It can also help build trust within the profession and create a culture of accountability. By following a code of conduct, financial crime professionals can demonstrate their commitment to upholding high standards of integrity and professionalism. This can make them more attractive to employers and enhance their reputation in the field. Additionally, codes of conduct often provide training resources and support mechanisms, which can be helpful for career growth. Financial crime professionals interested in developing their skills would do well to explore the codes of conduct relevant to their field.

Financial crime professionals need to maintain high standards of ethics and integrity to protect the industry's reputation. A code of conduct can be a valuable tool for achieving this goal. By following the guidelines in a code of conduct, professionals can demonstrate their commitment to upholding the highest standards of integrity and professionalism. This can make them more attractive to employers and enhance their reputation in their field.

CHAPTER 11

Internal Accountability

INTERNAL accountability holds employees and organizations responsible for their actions within an organization. This includes everything from financial fraud prevention to money laundering prevention, as well as other financial crimes.

One of the most important aspects of a financial crime prevention programme is internal accountability. Everyone in the organization must be aware of their responsibilities and adhere to the established policies and procedures. Management must provide adequate resources, including training, to ensure that employees effectively carry out their duties. It is also critical that individuals who identify potential or actual violations report them promptly to be addressed.

Internal accountability is essential for protecting an organization from financial crime losses, but it also helps promote a culture of compliance, reducing the chances of future incidents. By establishing clear lines of responsibility and encouraging employees to raise any concerns, organizations can create an environment where doing the right thing is the norm. This not only benefits the company financially but also helps to protect its reputation.

WHY INTERNAL ACCOUNTABILITY MATTERS

A financial crime professional's success depends on their ability to maintain a high level of internal accountability. This means adhering to the highest standards of ethics and integrity and being willing to hold themselves accountable for their actions. They can build trust with their colleagues and superiors by doing so, which is essential in this field. Maintaininga strong sense of internal accountability also helps protect them against corruption and other forms of wrongdoing.

Internal accountability is critical in financial crime investigations, money-laundering prevention, and other areas of finance. It may be even more important in these fields, as the potential consequences of misconduct are often much more significant. A financial crime professional who fails to uphold the highest standards can do severe damage to their organization and may even be responsible for economic losses.

It is therefore essential for anyone in a financial crime-related field to maintain a strong sense of internal accountability. By doing so, they can help protect themselves, their colleagues, and their organization from wrongdoing. And that is something we can all agree is essential.

Internal accountability is critical for protecting an organization from financial losses, but it also benefits. By holding employees accountable for their actions, organizations can improve compliance with applicable laws and regulations, reduce the chances of future incidents, and create a culture where doing the right thing is the norm. This not only protects the company financially but also its reputation.

HOW TO ESTABLISH AN EFFECTIVE INTERNAL ACCOUNTABILITY PROGRAMME

There are many ways to establish an effective internal accountability programme. One of the most important things is to have clear lines of responsibility and encourage employees to raise any concerns. Organizations can also promote a culture of compliance by establishing standards of conduct and providing training on identifying potential financial crimes.

It is also essential to have a system in place to investigate allegations of misconduct and hold those responsible accountable. This helps ensure that anyone who commits wrongdoing will be held accountable and sends a message that such behaviour will not be tolerated.

Establishing an effective internal accountability programme takes time and effort, but it is well worth it in the long run. By doing so, you can help protect your organization from financial crime losses and create a culture of compliance.

THE BENEFITS OF A STRONG INTERNAL ACCOUNTABILITY PROGRAMME

When it comes to preventing and investigating financial crimes, having a solid internal accountability programme is vital. This means that your company has in place systems and procedures that hold employees accountable for their actions. Such a system can help deter crime and identify and investigate any criminal activity.

A robust internal accountability programme should include the following:

- Clear policies and procedures detailing what is expected of employees
- Appropriate training on how to recognize and report financial crime
- Robust reporting mechanisms, including hotlines for employees to report suspicious activity anonymously
- Frequent audits to ensure compliance with policies and procedures
- Improved compliance with applicable laws and regulations
- Reduced chances of future incidents
- A culture where doing the right thing is the norm

These benefits are essential, but the last one is perhaps the most important — a culture where doing the right thing is the norm. When employees feel like they will be held accountable for their actions, they are less likely to engage in misconduct. This helps protect not just the organization financially but also its reputation. Establishing an effective internal accountability programme is one of the best ways to create such a culture.

TIPS FOR IMPLEMENTING AND MAINTAINING YOUR SUCCESSFUL PROGRAMME

So, how do you implement and maintain your own successful internal accountability programme? Here are a few tips:

- **Start with the basics.** Ensure that your policies and procedures are clear and concise and that employees have adequate training to recognize and report the financial crime.

- **Use effective reporting mechanisms.** Hotlines are an excellent way to encourage employees to report suspicious activity anonymously, without fear of reprisal.

- **Conduct frequent audits.** Audits help ensure compliance with policies and procedures and applicable laws and regulations.

- **Encourage employee engagement.** Promote a culture where doing the right thing is the norm by holding managers accountable for their team's actions, celebrating whistle-blowers, etc.

By following these tips, you can create and maintain a successful internal accountability programme that will help protect your organization from financial crime.

CHAPTER 12

External Accountability

E XTERNAL accountability is a system in which an organization is answerable to outside parties for its actions. This can include government entities, customers, or other interested groups. External accountability can help ensure that organizations act ethically and in the best interests of their stakeholders.

One of the most critical aspects of external accountability is transparency. Organizations should be open and honest about their activities, and they should be willing to share information with those who have a stake in them. This includes making financial reports available, disclosing details on investigations, and explaining decisions made by the organization.

External accountability can help organizations stay out of trouble, but it can also help improve them. When stakeholders are aware of what an organization is doing, they can provide feedback that can help the organization improve its operations. This type of feedback can be precious for organizations working to address unethical behaviour or financial crimes.

Organizations that embrace external accountability will likely find themselves better positioned to succeed both ethically and financially.

THE BENEFITS OF EXTERNAL ACCOUNTABILITY

Many financial crime professionals work in isolation and may not have regular contact with their peers. While this can be beneficial for creativity and problem solving, it can also lead to a lack of external accountability.

This can be dangerous, leading to complacency and a feeling of invincibility. Therefore, financial crime professionals need to have a strong network of colleagues that they can turn to for advice and feedback. A professional organization or trade association can be a great way to connect with other financial crime professionals, exchange ideas, and learn from others' experiences.

There are many benefits to external accountability, including:

Improved ethical behaviour: When professionals are held accountable by their peers, they are more likely to act ethically and follow the law.

Better financial performance: When professionals are held accountable, they are more likely to take their work seriously and make sure that they meet all the requirements expected of them.

Reduced risk of fraud: When individuals know that others monitor their actions, they are less likely to engage in fraudulent behaviour.

Greater transparency: When individuals and organizations are held accountable, it leads to greater transparency and helps to prevent corruption.

Results in more practical studies: When professionals are aware that their actions are being monitored, they are less likely to engage in criminal activity. This can help to improve the overall quality of financial crime investigations.

Stronger relationships with stakeholders: One of the critical goals of financial crime professionals is to build strong relationships with their stakeholders. When professionals are held accountable, it can help to strengthen these relationships and improve communication between all parties involved.

Each of these benefits is important in its own individual way, but they all work together to create a strong foundation for an organization. When organizations embrace external accountability, they become more accountable to their stakeholders and also improve their operations. This leads to a better reputation for the organization, which can help it achieve its goals both ethically and financially.

TYPES OF ORGANIZATIONS THAT CAN PROVIDE EXTERNAL ACCOUNTABILITY

Many different types of organizations can provide external responsibility for financial crime professionals. Some of the most common include:

Professional organizations: One of the best ways to connect with other financial crime professionals is through a professional organization. These organizations offer a variety of resources, including networking opportunities, educational programmes, and job boards. Many professional organizations also have ethics codes that members must abide by.

Trade associations: Trade associations are another great way to connect with others in your field. They typically offer various beneficial services, including education, advocacy, and networking events. Trade associations can also help develop industry-specific knowledge.

Regulatory agencies: Regulatory agencies play an essential role inholding individuals and organizations accountable. They are responsible for enforcing regulations and investigating allegations of wrongdoing. Regulatory agencies can provide several resources, including guidance documents, training programmes, and information about investigations.

Professional review organizations: Professional review organizations are another option for financial crime professionals who want to be held accountable. These organizations evaluate the performance of individual professionals and offer feedback. This can help professionals improve their skills and make sure that they comply with applicable laws and regulations.

Each of these options has its benefits, so it is essential to choose one that fits your needs. Professional organizations, trade associations, and regulatory agencies are all excellent choices for connecting with others in their field. If you are looking for more formal accountability, then professional review organizations may be a good option for you. Whichever route you choose, make sure that the organization is reputable and has a robust code of ethics.

External accountability is an essential part of any financial crime prevention strategy. When individuals and organizations are held accountable, it leads to greater transparency and helps to prevent corruption. Additionally, more effective investigations can be conducted when professionals know that their actions are being monitored. Finally, stronger relationships with stakeholders can be developed when professionals are held accountable. Each of these benefits is important in its way, and they all work together to create a strong foundation for an organization. Choose an external accountability option that fits your needs and get started today!

HOW TO CHOOSE AN ORGANIZATION FOR EXTERNAL ACCOUNTABILITY

When looking for an organization to provide external accountability, you should consider a few things. First, make sure that the organization is reputable, respected and has a strong code of ethics. Second, determine what type of services the organization offers. Third, decide what kind of support you need from the organization. Fourth, ask if the organization has any resources that could be helpful for you, such as training programmes or guidance documents. Finally, find out how much the organization costs to be involved with and whether discounts are available.

Choosing an external accountability option can be difficult, but it is essential to do your research before deciding. Many different organizations offer various services, so take your time and find one that fits your needs.

THE STEPS INVOLVED IN SETTING UP A RELATIONSHIP WITH AN ORGANIZATION FOR EXTERNAL ACCOUNTABILITY

Once you have chosen an organization for external accountability, the next step is to set up a relationship with them. This usually involves signing a contract and paying any associated fees. In some cases, you may also be required to provide certain information or documents.

The process of setting up a relationship can vary from organization to organization, so it is essential to read the instructions carefully. Make sure that you understand what is expected of you and how the relationship will work. If there are any questions, do not hesitate to contact the organization's customer service department.

Setting up a relationship with an external accountability organization is essential in creating a solid financial crime prevention strategy. By working with an established organization, you can ensure that your team has access to the latest information and resources. Additionally, you will be held accountable to high standards of ethics and professionalism.

CHAPTER 13

Ethical Leadership

MANY of us have had ethical leadership in our personal lives – while others may have lacked it in their professional careers. The kind of leadership style used will be determined by who is at the organization's top. Ethical leaders give way to employees through inspiration, training, and fostering a culture of trust and respect.

WHAT IS ETHICAL LEADERSHIP?

Ethical leadership entails demonstrating acceptable behaviour both inside and outside the workplace, and following established principlesand values.

Ethical leadership is about demonstrating solid moral principles that will point out wrongdoings (even when it may not benefit their company) and showing what's right at the heart of being an ethical leader. Ethical leaders set the example for the rest of the organization, expecting their employees to acknowledge and follow their actions and words with equal conviction.

We could also argue that we encounter numerous unethical leadership in today's political and business leaders. Still, many excellent examples of executives and politicians have utilized ethical leadership to propel their success.

THE IMPORTANCE OF ETHICAL LEADERSHIP

Ethical leadership has several advantages that have been researched and documented by clinical researchers and mentioned in many excellent business success stories. Here are some examples of the benefits of ethical leadership:

Improved brand image: When a company is run with strong ethical values and leadership, it will be reflected in the brand image. Consumers are more likely to do business with companies they believe have sound moral principles.

Increased productivity: Employees who feel that their leaders behave ethically are more productive. They trust their leaders, feel valued, and want to help the organization succeed. This positive attitude contributes to lower staff turnover rates and reduced absenteeism.

Reduced legal costs: When organizations adhere to high ethical standards, they are less likely to find themselves in legal trouble. Studies have shown that businesses with solid ethics systems experience fewer lawsuits and regulatory actions against them than those without such systems in place.

Improved employee morale: A happy workforce is a productive one. Employees who believe in the ethical values of their company and feel that they are being treated fairly by their leaders are more likely to be satisfied with their jobs. This can lead to reduced stress levels and better attendance.

Better decision-making: Ethical leaders make better decisions because they consider all possible consequences before acting. They also have a strong sense of right and wrong, which helps them face difficult choices with a clear moral compass.

Greater employee engagement: When employees feel like they are part of something larger than themselves – when they share the same values as their organization – they are more engaged in their work. These employees are more productive at work and stay within organizations longer.

Improved customer service: Customers prefer to do business with companies they trust. When a company has strong ethical values and leadership, its customers can be assured that they deal with honourable people who behave fairly and honestly in all dealings.

There are many advantages to employing ethical leadership within an organization. By following the principles of ethical leadership, companies can improve their brand image, increase productivity, reduce legal costs, boost employee morale, make better decisions, achieve greater employee engagement, and provide superior customer service.

ETHICAL LEADERSHIP PRINCIPLES

We have discussed a lot about ethical leadership, but there's a framework that must be followed for it to have any meaning. The most popular term used to describe the principles of ethical leadership is FATHER, which we will now deconstruct:

Fairness: Fairness is a value that runs through all of ethics. Fairness involves how people interact with one another and expect to be treated. We hope to be treated fairly, and in return, we treat others fairly. There is no room for favouritism in fairness when everyone is treated equally, and equality is also associated with handling a situation. If two people make the same mistake, they should be penalized in the same way.

Accountability: It is good to be held accountable for poor judgments and mistakes; this is another critical quality of ethical leadership. Some of us like to forget about our errors as soon as possible, while others prefer to point the finger at someone else or even the gods. However, admitting responsibility for a blunder demonstrates that you are a robust and well-rounded leader who people would want to follow.

Transparency: Transparency is the act of being completely open and honest with all stakeholders. Transparent leaders will share everything – the good, bad, and ugly – with those who need to know, including employees, customers, suppliers, and investors. This builds trust between leaders and followers as they realize that they are not hiding anything from them.

Responsibility: Leaders must take responsibility for their actions and decisions. They cannot pass the buck or blame someone else when things go wrong; instead, they shoulder the blame and work to fix the situation. Responsibility also includes being proactive in preventing unethical behaviour from happening in the first place.

Trust: You cannot have a fantastic team without trust pervading it. How can you be expected to do work if you do not trust that your team won't steal it or claim it as their own, among other things? We demand that individuals around us trust and grow high-performing teams, whether in the military, sports teams, or corporate groups.

Honesty: We all appreciate it when people are honest with us, so what happens when our leaders are? It creates an atmosphere in which we can freely talk about important issues. This feeds into trust, and if you cannot be honest with someone, then faith is lost, and you won't hear the truth in that debate.

Equality: There has been a lot of debate about equality in our contemporary society, but it is the foundation on which we survive and are happy. No one wants to be considered inferior, and discriminating against various things has no effect on our survival or pleasure.

Discrimination is a red flag that you are dealing with someone who isn't well-rounded, ethical, or moral. Working with principled leaders ensures that the playing field is level in their eyes, and as a result, it creates an attitude that treats these concerns with the same amount of importance across the team.

Respect: We all want to be respected by those around us, and it is a key ingredient in any healthy relationship. Leaders who respect their followers will earn their trust and admiration. This goes beyond just the spoken words; leaders must also act respectfully. For example, they should never belittle someone or embarrass them publicly.

These principles work together to create an ethical leadership framework that anyone in any field of work can use. When we adhere to these principles, our teams operate more effectively and efficiently, reducing legal costs, boosting employee morale, making better decisions, achieving greater employee engagement, and providing superior customer service. Remember: always put the needs of others before your own and practice fairness in all you do!

TRAITS OF ETHICAL LEADERS

There are certain traits that ethical leaders tend to have. Here are a few of them:

Sets a great example: One of the most crucial elements of ethical leadership is to walk the walk and talk the talk. An ethical leader sets high standards for their team, just like they do for themselves daily. Would they complete the work that they are requesting someone else to perform? Yes should be the automatic response.

Respects everyone equally: Another aspect of ethical leadership is maintaining gratitude for others, the team and organization. Another indicator of ethical leadership is respect for others, equal treatment for everyone in the team, and a firm adherence to high standards. Being attentive, sympathetic, giving voice to opposing views, and valuing peoples' work equally are all qualities that ethical leaders have.

Open communication: Being a good communicator is also an indication of an ethical leader. Being a good, transparent communicator is sometimes taken for granted. This communication must flow down from the top in day-to-day discussions to help build trust and respect for one another.

Fair mediation: The ability to arbitrate disputes is also an essential component of ethical leadership. It is critical to be impartial, listen to both sides, and come up with compromises that satisfy both parties. In a more equitable approach, the treatment of others while maintaining an equal position is essential.

Effective stress management: Leaders with a high ethical standard must deal with stressful workplace situations. These teams are generally successful and require continual praise and appreciation for the task at hand. One of the essential qualities of an ethical leader is the ability to manage tense situations by keeping cool under pressure and paying close attention to the team when things are starting to boil over. Being a positive influence while also creating an atmosphere of fairness and trust can assist you.

Adapts to change: The ability to listen to others and discover standard solutions that work for the benefit of all team members rather than just one person at a time is crucial to ethical leadership. Change may come upon a company, a community, or even a team without notice – or with too much warning.

Ethical leadership entails listening to and addressing concerns while also making decisions that must be completed and respected by the whole team. Working in new locations and conditions is possible at any time, and an ethical leader can aid with the transition.

Zero tolerance of ethical violations: Ethical leaders hold themselves to account daily; therefore, it is all about doing the correct things at the appropriate times – not only when it is convenient or when someone is watching. This is why being held accountable and preventing others from breaching ethical standards of conduct is so important.

ETHICAL LEADERSHIP EXAMPLES

There are many different types of ethical leadership, but the most common example is a parent. Parents must set boundaries and be consistent in their actions to ensure that their children learn right from wrong. This can also be said for teachers, coaches, and other adult authority figures.

Another great example of ethical leadership would be Dr. Martin Luther King Jr., who showed exceptional courage in the face of adversity while advocating for civil rights across America. He inspired others to stand against discrimination and violence through his words and actions, setting an excellent example for future generations.

Finally, one more great example of ethical leadership comes from Mahatma Gandhi. After years of peaceful protests and civil disobedience against British rule in India, Gandhi eventually led his country to independence. He is remembered for his philosophy of nonviolent resistance, which inspired many other movements worldwide.

These individuals exhibited exceptional ethics and led by example, setting the bar high for those who followed them. As an ethical leader, it is essential to learn from their examples and strive to emulate their virtues in your own work life. Doing so will help build trust and respect within your team, laying a solid foundation for success.

HOW TO DEVELOP THE SKILLS NEEDED TO BE AN ETHICAL LEADER

You will need to establish a few essential skills to be an effective, ethical leader. The first is listening and understanding others, compromising, and finding standard solutions. You must also be able to handle stress effectively and lead by example.

If you are looking to improve your skills in these areas, you can do several different things. First, try attending workshops or seminars on leadership development. There are often many other courses available, which will allow you to learn from experienced professionals. Alternatively, read books or articles on the topic, or take online courses.

Another great way to develop your skills as an ethical leader is through practice. Try different role-playing scenarios with your team, or create ethical dilemmas that you can solve together. This will help you better understand the complexities of making tough decisions and allow you to test out different solutions.

Finally, it is essential to be aware of your values and principles and always stay true to them. Live by example and hold yourself accountable for your actions. If you have a strong sense of ethics and are committed to leading ethically, you will be able to succeed in the field of financial crime prevention.

ETHICAL CHALLENGES AND HOW TO DEAL WITH THEM

One of the most important aspects of being a financial crime professional is upholding high ethical standards. This can be difficult, especially when investigating crimes and tracking down criminals. You may be tempted to cut corners or take shortcuts, but it is crucial to remember that your integrity is at stake. If you compromise your ethics, you could lose the trust of others in the field, which would damage your career.

Another challenge faced by financial crime professionals is dealing with sensitive information. You may come across confidential data while investigating cases, and it is essential to protect this information from being leaked. Otherwise, you could jeopardize ongoing investigations and put people's safety at risk. It can be difficult to keep secrets, but it is essential to do so to maintain your work's integrity.

These are just a few of the ethical and professional challenges financial crime professionals face. It is essential to be aware of these challenges and to have the courage to face them head-on. With diligence and perseverance, you can overcome any obstacle in your way and succeed in this exciting field.

How to Deal with Them

There are several ways to deal with a financial crime professionals' ethical and professional challenges. First, you need to be aware of these challenges and understand why they exist. This will help you stay focused and motivated during difficult times.

Second, you need to maintain high standards of ethics and professionalism at all times. This means following the rules and regulations set out by your organization, as well as behaving in a responsible manner both on and off the job.

Finally, you need to be prepared to face any challenge that comes your way. You can do this by staying up-to-date on current trends and developments in the field of financial crime. With knowledge and experience under your belt, you will be ready for anything that comes your way.

These are just a few tips for dealing with the ethical and professional challenges financial crime professionals face. By following these guidelines, you can overcome any obstacle in your way and succeed in this exciting field.

CONCLUSION

The takeaway from our look at ethical leadership is that organizations need to have a clear code of conduct and a philosophy of ethical behaviour. Leaders within the organization need to be held accountable to these codes, and external stakeholders (customers and investors) need to feel confident that the company is behaving ethically. Organizations that can demonstrate their commitment to ethics through transparent financial reporting are less likely to experience negative consequences in the event of a financial crime.

www.ingramcontent.com/pod-product-compliance
Lightning Source LLC
Chambersburg PA
CBHW070455220526
45466CB00004B/1838